Fortune Cookies

Volume 7

Dr. Kareem Pottinger

YSD Publishing House

Library of Congress Catalog in
Publication Data

YSD PUBLISHING HOUSE
14490 Coastal Bay Circle 13204
Naples, FL. 34119

Library of Congress Catalog Card
Number:
2013934185
International Standard Book
Number 978-1-937171-06-3

Dedicated to my firstborn

YOUNGSABATH POTTINGER

If I ever leave this planet, I have
always kept you in mind.

Not leavening my wisdom far behind

Grow Good

INTRODUCTION

The true intent of this book
was to write a set of guidelines
that could be
immediately implemented in
the progress and advancement
of my sons elite
life.
This vast deep knowledge was
to be used as a
tool
to keep him far beyond just,
"ahead of the learning curb" for
lack of better expression.
These
rules are the widely accepted
and used unspoken
secrets amongst the elite in
which we use to rear our

young.
Although these are our
secrets
and most of us will and should
be extremely displeased for
having them on display for the
"normal's" of the world to
receive, I decided to release
them nevertheless.
For,
upon reading the finished
piece I realized that these elite
secrets
could not only serve to benefit
my son and family to come
well, but that the entire
world
could serve to benefit from
these lists of guidelines.
The way that this book is
intended to be received is to

ponder upon each page for a
complete 24 hours.
Each page is to be pondered
upon for the whole day; it is to
be used as topic of discussion
for that day amongst peers,
friends, and family members'
etcetera.
It is especially designed to be
pondered upon mostly by you.
For a complete 24 hours deep
thought on each subject
should be pondered upon. The
reason being is to see how
these guidelines could
be
implemented into your current
life,
how should they have been
implemented in your past
life, and how can they benefit
your future.

It
is only through the true
belief
and usage of these
guidelines
that your life's
works will be greatly
affected
in its progress.

*Even when
you are
going
through
your
hell
an
angel
will
sometimes
make an
appearance*

*When you are
better,
it
doesn't
matter
if
you are
out-numbered
by
the
competition
or not*

*It will benefit
you to acquire a
taste for
independence
because
it is
the
spirit
that drives
the world's
most
successful*

*The way to
win a
conflict
with your
rival
is
by
breaking
the
will
of
your rival*

On your way to the top, it is extremely important that you never forget where you came from because it will make it a lot easier for you not to get lost

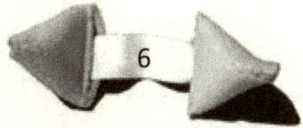

*When your
infrastructure
is
ready
for
anything,
you
will
be
ready
for
anything*

*You
should
always
take
full
advantage
of
any
openings
presented*

*It will
be a
benefit
for you
to
make the
enemy
of
your
enemy
become
your friend*

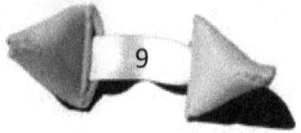

*In life; you have
to meet your
vision
and in order for
you to meet
your vision,
you will have
to
perform
some form
of
action*

*It is not
just
about
reaching
your
goals,
it is
also
about
accomplishing
your
dreams*

Don't ever forget that some people will ruin your agenda just because they are bored

*Before you are
to begin any of
your
projects,
you
should always
make sure that
the
project
has any
real-merit
to it*

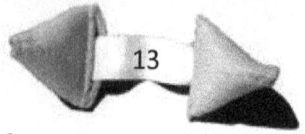

Learn when to speak at the right time because when you do speak at the right time, your words will hold more weight

*Be prepared
when defeating
the people with
a lot of
pride and ego;
because of the
fact that
they do not
like to lose,
they will
always come
back*

*Your
actions
moving
forward
should
be
your
main
concern*

*In business;
you should
always try
to get the
best
amount of
value
for the
least
amount
of
dollar*

*You
should
never
stay
involved
with
something
that
you
are
miserable
in*

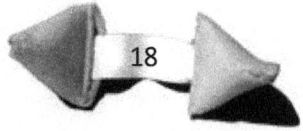

*Slow-progress
is
lasting
progress,
and
rapid
expansion
can
leave
you
in
massive-default*

*Never give-up
on
yourself;
there
is
opportunity
everywhere,
you
just have to
look
for
it*

*You can not
force
someone
to fall in
love
with you
but
you
can
increase
your
odds*

*Sometimes
things
have
to
fall-apart
so
that
better-things
can
fall
into
place*

Some of the most successful relationships are based on lies and deceit, so don't be fooled by one of the most common illusions

*Always keep in
mind that
when
making
deals
they
do
have
the
ability
to
change*

*You will
never
be able
to
move-on
with
one
foot
stuck
in
the
door*

In any accomplishment that you are trying to achieve; you have to be willing to fall, but when you do fall just make sure that you are falling forward

*The things
that are
true
in
life
will never
change,
and
they will
always
remain
true*

Some people
are
so far
behind in
the
race
that they
actually
think that
they are
winning the
race

*When you
want
to
determine
the
behavior
of the
people,
look at the
behavior
of
their leader*

*The
safest
accidents,
are
the
ones
that
never
happen*

*You cannot
leave your life
up to
fortune;
every piece of
effort
that you
put into your
life counts,
it will all
add-up
in the end*

Don't ever forget that even the person that is clean can quickly fall into the mud

*When you
believe
in
yourself
it makes it
a lot
easier for
other people
to
believe
in
you*

When trying to attain great-success; sometimes you will have to take great-risk while never looking back and regretting a thing

When you want to become better, you are going to have to go after bigger

The people that are in your life who are not being genuine because they are trying to achieve a certain thing in which they need you to attain it, will always turn their back on you; this is how you will know that they are fake, so pay close attention

In
your lifetime
the
relationships
that you are
involved in will
come and go
because that is
what they do,
everyone in life
is on their own
path

*Sometimes a
person needs
to be
more selfish
for
themselves
in order
to get to
where they
really would
like to
be*

*Remember that
your
repetition
will
create
a
pattern
that
everyone
else
can
see*

The players of a game may change but when the game that is being played remains a constant, the game in it of itself will always remain the same

*It is
extremely-wise
to
stay
away
from
trouble
because
trouble
will
always
cost you*

*In many cases;
you will
have to be
quicker
with
the
second-stroke
or
longer
with
the
first*

*The people
that are
fake
will
always
turn
their
back
on
you
so
pay-attention*

When someone is attempting to deceive you; always remember that deceptions sole purpose is to hide, so you should be more focused on what is this person trying to hide instead of the deceit in it of itself

*Many people
in this
world
have the
persona of a
wild-elephant
and
wild-elephants
cannot
be
reasoned
with*

*Through
birth
and
rebirth
we
hope
to
learn
from
our
inherited
mistakes*

Without the proper upkeep of yourself, you are and will become your own problems

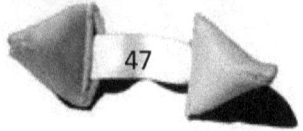

You
don't
abandon
a whole
mission
because
of a
few
bugs,
you
fix
them

No operation goes directly as planned

You should never try and force things to make sense; when things do not make sense, it is because that thing that does not make sense is not true

*Everything that
you try to
accomplish in
life
has mostly
to do
with
the
ability
of
your
thought-process*

50

*In order
to
become a
winner
you have to
learn how
not
to
be
defeated
so
easily*

An advantage that fails you, you need to eliminate

*You must
solve
your
problems
from
their
roots-end
or else
they will
just
pop
back-up*

Some people in this world need to be considered as a dragon and when dancing with a dragon; forget the rules of engagement and it will devour you

*You
never
know
how
long
a
good-deal
will
last
so
take
advantage*

*Your life
will
turn-out
the
absolute
exact
way
that
you
set-it-up
to
turn-out*

When attempting to become victorious in your endeavors, you have to put in the work

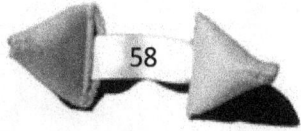

*Your mind
is
your
truest-friend
and a
truest-friend
is the friend
that you
should
always
listen
to*

*Understanding
the fact that
while a
concept
doesn't change
it can
evolve,
will always
keep you
progressing
in that
concept*

When an operation does not go directly as planned, you calm down and tie-up loose ends

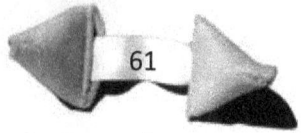

*Always try to
do
better
regardless
if your
perfect
or
not and you
will always be
performing
at your
optimum-level*

*Your life will
come at you
fast
and
disappear right
in front
of you,
when you
are
not
paying
attention*

*The
good
will
only
outweigh
the
bad,
when
it
needs
to*

Planning
will
be
the
key
to
your
life's
wants
and
wishes

*You should
always
have
an
exit-plan
in
whatever
it is
that
you
are
doing*

Sometimes it will take; the worst-things to happen to you, in order for you to see what is really going on

*Live
for
yourself,
if not
then you run
the risk
of
becoming
a
very
unhappy
elderly*

The
best-way
for
you
to
learn
is
for you
to get
out there
and
do

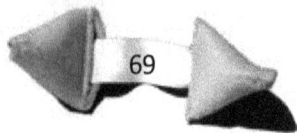

Be careful
of
only
focusing
on
one-piece
of the puzzle
when
there
is
a
bigger-picture

*Never
rule
out
anything
just
because
you
think
that
it
doesn't
happen*

*In whatever it
is that you are
doing,
you should
always make
sure that you
do not miss an
opportunity
to
pivot
into something
greater*

Most
"want to bee's"
while
messing-up,
will
pick-up
speed very
quickly
and the reason
why is because
at least their
trying

*Whosoever
has
the
money
will
have
the
power
at
some
point*

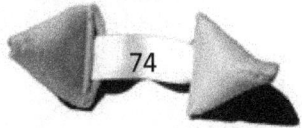

*You
will
never
know
for
yourself
until
you
try
for
yourself*

*When you
set out
to do something
and you get it
done,
there will
always be a
sense of
accomplishment
that
comes along
with it*

*The cleansing
of your
negative
feelings
and
the washing of
your wounds
is
extremely-vital
towards
moving
forward*

Don't ever
forget
that it will
always
be
up to
you
to take
care of
yourself
in this
life

Anything in this world
is possible
for you to
accomplish but
it will be up to
you
to break
those invisible
chains
that are holding
you back

*The
only
way for you
to
protect
your
dream,
is for
you
to
follow
your dream*

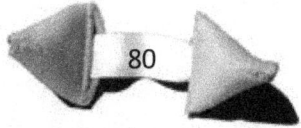

*What you do
now and the
choices
that you make
will
dictate
how the rest
of
your
life
will
become*

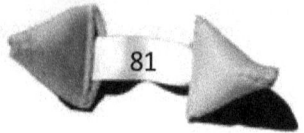

*Do
not
settle
for
pretty
when
you
can
become
gorgeous*

*Over
doing
is
exactly
equal
to
wasting
time*

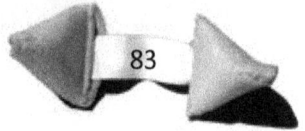

The way that you respond to your roadblocks is exactly what will determine your future

*In this world
you
get
what you
create
and
you will
also
look like
who
you
become*

*Learn
how
to
take
the
best
from
your
situations
and
keep things
moving forward*

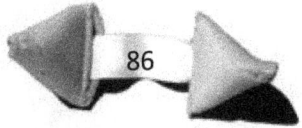

*Learn to
look
at your
life
like you are the
designer
of it
and then figure
out
how you would
like it to
look*

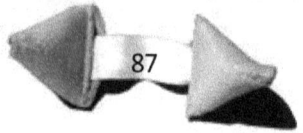

*Your
real-agenda in
any situation
should be
what
you're not
feeling,
not
what
you
are
feeling*

In the mist
of
accomplishing
all your
task,
forgetting
to
stay
focused
can easily
be
done

In order to avoid deluding yourself, it is a constant must that you occasionally take a step back and look at who you are on a grander-scope

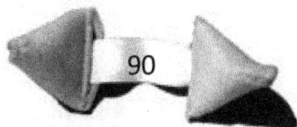

Once you have achieved the level of consciousness of being constantly aware of which direction your life is heading, the more direct control over it you will have

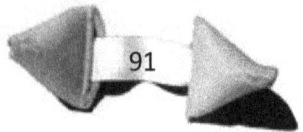

*Do
everything
that you
should be
doing
in order
to
make-it
and
you
will
make-it*

*Making a
plan
is
all
about
figuring-out
what
steps
need
to
be
taken-first*

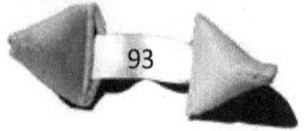

*You need to
hold yourself
accountable
for your
decisions
and
the
circumstances
that you
find
yourself
in*

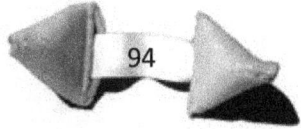

*The willingness
never to
give-up
combined with
the ability to
work really
hard
not to let
yourself down,
will get you far
in this
life*

*Sometimes
your
point of you
view
may not
be the
one
that
needs
to
be
heard*

*Nothings
ever
to
beautiful
or
expensive
for you to
possess, should
always be your
attitude
and
opinion*

*It is very
important
when
making
a
plan
to make sure
that your
plan
has
no
weaknesses*

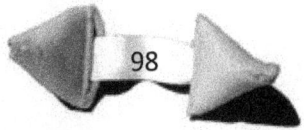

*If its
out there
for you
to
reach it,
grab it,
and
touch it,
then
take
full
advantage*

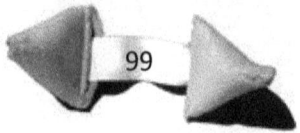

*Adding an
editing-process
to your
life
will make
everything
a lot
simpler
and
easier
for
you*

*You
have to learn
how to
stand-up
for yourself
if
you
would like to
become
someone
substantial
in life*

*Being
better
will
always
cost
more*

*There
is
no
stumbling
when
your
steps
are
true*

*A
quitter
will
always
walk
away
from
their
obligations;
pay
attention*

*Instead
of seeing what
they want you
to see, you
have to open
your
mind's-eye
to the many
different
possibilities
that are always
out there*

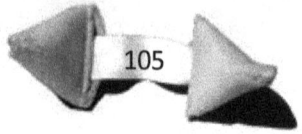

When the
chips
are
down,
a good sense of
humor and a
good
attitude
is
vital
to
survival

*Absorb it
and
acknowledge it
but
keep it moving
because
you
have
other
things
to
do*

*You
have to
change
with
the
times
or run the
risk
of
getting
left
behind*

You
must remember
that the people
who are
ahead
of you already
know what
they are
going
to
do
next

The people who are better don't really need to compete

Having money will always be easier than not having it

*Not
one
person
respects
a
quitter;
not
even
one*

Sometimes others can see what we do not see,
which is why it is important to ask for advice when your answer is not obvious

113

*Stay
focused
on
your
goal
and
one-day
you
will
achieve
it*

*Sometimes
all you need
to do is
allow people
time and
they
might
change
the
way
they
feel*

*People
will
always
only
see
what
they
choose
to
look
for*

*When it is
necessary
for you
to
speak to
someone in
order to get
things
accomplished,
make sure you
speak to a
decision-maker*

*A
thief
can
only
steal
what you
leave
available
for
them
to
steal*

*To
defeat
your
opponent
you
must
first
take
care
of
yourself*

The only
way to
break-down
barriers
between you
and another is
to have
everything
out
in
the
open

*It is
one thing
to look
at the
grey-spaces
in the
world,
it is a total
different-thing
to
actually live
in them*

*Sometimes
you need
an
outsiders
perspective
when
making
a
decision;
fresh-eyes
never
hurt*

*Only
take
people
as
they are,
not how
you
would
like
them
to
be*

*The mistakes
that you have
made in the
past will
become
your
guidelines
and
wisdom
of
the
future*

*Why
pay
attention
to
things
that
are
being
removed
through
evolutionary
growth*

*Always
remember that
when you
try and control
too much,
it can
allow you to
lose
focus
on what
your
point of view is*

*Before
you
can
expect
to
grow,
you
have
to
perfect
the
basics*

When you put
yourself into a
situation
to win
from
the
beginning,
you will
win
in
the
end

*It is much easier
to receive
love
when you are
winning rather
than when you
are losing
because everyone
loves a winner,
but the love that
you receive when
you are losing is
one of the
strongest-loves*

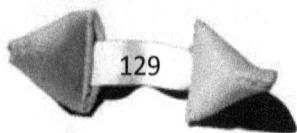

*It's ironic
how
the
truths
are
sometimes
harder
to
absorb
than
the
lies*

*Always
remember
when dealing
with people
that they are
the way they
are because of
the experiences
that they
have lived
and
been-through*

*The
purpose
of
life
is to have
abundance
of the
things
you
want
and
like*

In life you must never lose-track of those things that cause your resources to be taken away from your goals

*The
outcome
of a
person's life
will always
be
determined
by
the
decisions
that they
make*

*When
you
work
and
believe
hard
enough,
progression
happens*

*When
over-working
yourself; in
order to
equal
out the balance
you
have to
set aside
time
too
play-hard*

*The
steadiness
of
your
purpose
is
what
will
maintain
your
progression*

*When
it's
worth
all
or
nothing,
you
have to go
big
or
go
home*

*It is
very important
to enjoy
your
life
now and as
much as you
can
because
life is short
and time is
luck*

*When
too many
people
are
doing
the same
thing that you
are,
your
margins for
making a profit
lessens*

*Avoid making
decisions
when
desperate
or in a
rush because it
can lead you
to making
an
ill-advised
life
choice*

*Don't ever
forget
that there
is
more
than
one
way
to
spread
your
wings*

*When
you
make a
mistake,
focus
on
the
solutions
and
not
the
regrets*

You should always do what is best for you at the moment

*Leave yourself
with
multiple-options
and
you
will
always
have more
of a
chance
to
succeed*

*Take
care
of
your
old-problems
and
they
wont
blend-in
into
your
new-problems*

*If you
tell
them
you're
in
an
admirable
position,
they
might
admire
you*

*One
of
the
first-steps
to
evolving
as a
person
is to
stop
making
excuses*

*Be wary
of those that
cloud
the
water,
they
might
be
more
hurtful
than
helpful*

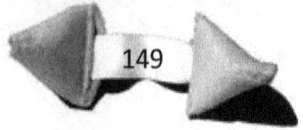

*Sometimes
in
life
you
have
to
slow-down
in
order
to
speed-up*

*Don't ever let
the
difference
of
opinion
get
in
the
way
of
the
end-product*

*When
you're always
trying
to do
the
wisest-thing
you
will always
be
doing
the
best-thing*

*In
this
life
it
is
your
job
to
evolve*

*A
winner
does
not
need
an
excuse*

*Change doesn't
happen
by itself, it is
important
for you to
realize
that very
little
will change
until you
change
it*

Trying to get
from point A
to
point B
in the least
amount
of
steps,
will always
produce the
most amount of
out-put

*It
will
never
be
about
the
process
once
the
results
are
outstanding*

*There is no time
to waste
in this short
lifespan
of ours,
so take the
first-step
towards
bringing your
dream
to life
today*

When assessing a judgment upon an individual; that judgment should be derived from the persons character and nothing else

The end

Additional books written by
Dr. Kareem Pottinger available online at
www.FORTUNECOOKIES.me
and your local book stores nationwide

<u>FORTUNE COOKIES VOLUMES 1-11</u>

   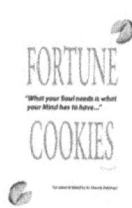

also   available   on   your

<u>Kindle</u>   <u>Nook</u>   <u>Apple</u>   <u>devices</u>